A CAT LOVER LIVES HERE

Don Cottrell

Copyright © Don Cottrell 2015
This book is sold subject to the condition that it shall not, by way of trade or otherwise, be lent, resold, hired out, or otherwise circulated without the publisher's prior consent in any form of binding or cover other than that in which it is published and without a similar condition including this condition being imposed on the subsequent publisher.
The moral right of Don Cottrell has been asserted.
ISBN-13: 978-1507679012
ISBN-10: 1507679017

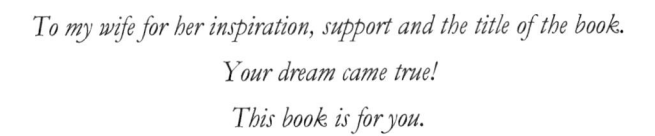

To my wife for her inspiration, support and the title of the book.
Your dream came true!
This book is for you.

CONTENTS

1. Strange Beginnings 1
2. The Cattery is Born 8
3. General Behaviour of Cats 12
4. Little Old Ladies 16
5. Tale of Blackie 23
6. Collection and Delivery 28
7. Cats and Their Strange Ways 32
8. Other Cat Habits 36
9. The Tale of Rupert and Perkins 41
10. Survivors 45
11. Favourites (Or What You Shouldn't Have) 48
12. The Other Side of the Coin 51

ACKNOWLEDGMENTS

There are two people who have been of invaluable help to me in producing this book.

Without Enid Cadman my scrawl could not have been transformed into legible form - thank you Enid.

My good friend Elwyn Harrison played 'Chinese Whispers' via the internet with the publisher to bring the project to fruition.

Thank you both.

1. Strange Beginnings

"Right, that's it! Everybody up, we are going home." This was the rude awakening on day three of our caravan holiday in Cornwall. A further surprise was that our children were delighted. The reason for this was simple - our three cats, Tabitha, Bootsie and Debbie were incarcerated in the feline equivalent of Colditz. They were there because our regular cattery had just closed, the owner being too ill to continue. Our cats had always been content there and in fact, when the owner went on holiday we had helped out, and so they knew they would be well cared for.

The next time we wanted a holiday we took the cats with us. This was not a resounding success! We were so afraid that if they went out from the caravan off their leads they would disappear forever that we all became paranoid. A solution had to be found. It was. At the bottom of our garden was an old pigeon loft which had been converted into a hen house when we had moved in with our nine chickens. By now, only Henrietta survived, and she had taken up residence in the greenhouse to live out her twilight years in comfort. The pigeon-loft hen house was soon scrubbed out and two spacious cages installed, one for Tabitha and her kitten Bootsie and the other for Debbie so that when we next wanted a holiday, into the cages they went and a friend could then easily look after them for us.

It will not take an intelligent reader long to realise what many of our friends soon realised. "Mimi and Don have got a couple of cages, they will look after 'Ginger', 'Whiskey', 'Fluffy' or whoever." Our local vet seemed to be involved in the plot, as was our friend, the ex-cattery owner. It became increasingly obvious that we were destined to become cattery owners in a small way. We telephoned the local Planning Department and their comment was that looking after half a dozen cats was of no more interest to them than someone letting a couple of rooms on a Bed and Breakfast basis. The official phrase was that it was 'de minimus'. Those were certainly the 'good old days' compared to the modern penchant for petty rules and regulations about almost every aspect of life.

Before closing this chapter it would seem appropriate to give a further account of the four beautiful ladies responsible in their different ways for the whole story. The most important, of course, is my wife. Like most husbands I was not totally aware of what I had let myself in for! I knew Mimi was as fond of animals as I was, and that she had also had many pets of her own, whereas I had not. I was also discovering that I was unable to refuse her anything!

Consequently within four months of our marriage we had acquired, during a visit to Devon, a Jack Russell puppy - we lived in a first floor flat in Liverpool for goodness sake! Furthermore, I was unaware that in less than six months we would move to live in Devon. I still do not know if Mimi knew this, guessed this, or as I now suspect, decided this. It matters not; within twelve months of our wedding we were living in a 16th Century house with about one quarter of an acre of garden in Brixham, South Devon. It was here that we first encountered Debbie as a very young cat.

One morning there she was on the doorstep and my reaction was quite logical - "She is probably just a bit lost, advertise her in the Post Office window and her owner will come for her."

"She can't stay here, you know how Oscar (the dog) hates cats, he will probably kill her!"

In the face of subtle pressure then my objections went as follows:

"Well, put her in the laundry room until the owner calls."

"Well, she can stay until the RSPCA come for her."

"You can try, but don't blame me if the dog hurts her."

"I'm surprised you haven't had more trouble with the dog."

And then, you've guessed it,

"Oh well, they seem to get on so well, and she is rather pretty, she may as well stay."

I had made the fatal capitulation, now the build up could begin.

Debbie was indeed a beautiful young tortie cat who responded to our care and grew into a very confident lady, who was aware of her beauty and her ability to have her way on almost all occasions. She was totally unafraid of Oscar, who became her greatest fan. She was a cat with a presence and a sense of humour!

In common with many folk in Devon in the early sixties we let some rooms in our house for Bed and Breakfast. The dining room had a French window onto the terrace along the back of the house, and Debbie's favourite sport in the mornings was to sit gazing pathetically out into the garden. The first guests down to breakfast would, of course, make a great fuss of her and kindly let her out onto the terrace. She would then walk along the terrace and leap in through the open kitchen window landing on the draining board and then make her way back to wait for the door into the dining room to open, whereupon she would re-enter the dining room to receive the adulation she felt was her due. Once satisfied that she had everyone's attention she would then proceed with the 'action replay' and graciously permit another unsuspecting guest to open the French window for her. Obviously, long-staying guests became familiar with her routine but such was her charm that they all played along.

She eventually received her comeuppance in the following way. The draining board she used as a landing pad was of pine, and every night it was scrubbed and placed outside to dry and air overnight. On the morning in question a combination of factors caused her discomfort. Firstly two guests had asked for early breakfasts before a fishing trip, and secondly early morning drizzle meant that the draining board was not in position. Debbie performed her 'I'm a pathetic cat that is not allowed out to play' routine, the guests duly a obliged with the French window, and she scampered along the terrace and leapt nimbly through the kitchen window only to disappear among the pots and pans stored in the cupboard below the now non-existent draining board! When we opened the door to this cupboard out walked a very subdued Miss Deborah. Out of kindness we managed not to laugh until she had quietly retired from the room but I am afraid she probably did hear the subsequent explosion of mirth in kitchen. Naturally the guests were intrigued and so had to be told but I must say everyone did their best to restore her dignity.

I had now become so enthralled with Debbie's antics that I was a 'pushover' when informed that we had a new kitten. Tabitha was a little tabby - quarter Siamese - from a litter belonging to a friend. She too, grew into a fascinating adult cat who from a very early age showed all the instincts of the excellent mother she eventually became. The first signs of her maternal nature showed up when we moved the hens from their summer quarters into the large store at the end of one wing of the house. The hens were confined in a deep litter system in the store but on warmer days when we were in the garden the boldest one, Henrietta, would fly over the half door and settle down with us hoping to scrounge some toast or cake. Once she was settled against the south facing wall in the late Autumn sun, Tabitha would lie alongside and give her a thorough wash.

Tabitha eventually produced five delightful kittens, four of which were very vigorous indeed, but the fifth was a poor little thing which seemed to be crippled and unable to stand. After some weeks the four were making great strides, but the smallest seemed not to be progressing at all and we decided to take it to the vet to be put to sleep. He, very wisely, told us that Tabitha must be convinced of its ultimate survival or she would have killed it at once. We, therefore, returned home having increased our knowledge of cats a little more. Tabitha was the most thorough and attentive mother you could wish for. We watched fascinated as she washed and cleaned the kittens so that they learned how to use the litter tray. She also taught them the skills of hunting, starting by bringing in a dead mouse. She then sat them all in a row and showed each kitten the victim. She then allowed each kitten, one at a time, to practice pouncing on it. We found it difficult sometimes to permit this but realised that it was the way of nature, which became more difficult to cope with when she brought in a live mouse for training purposes! Tabitha's confidence in the smallest kitten was justified, because although still small and slight, she turned out to be a most proficient hunter.

The four advanced kittens were all found loving homes and we decided to keep the baby. At this time there was a television programme all about National Service life. One of the characters played by the late Alfie Bass was supposed to have bad feet and was, therefore, 'excused boots'. His nickname was Bootsie and so this became the name of the kitten. It was, perhaps, not appropriate to her final slim, lissome elegance but it reminded us with affection of the little struggling creature we had watched blossom. As I have said, Bootsie became a proficient hunter and was the scourge of the rats who attempted to steal the stocks of chicken food. Sadly, perhaps because of her early struggles in life Bootsie did not survive as long as most cats, and had to be put to sleep by the vet who had encouraged us to keep her some ten years earlier.

These three I suppose, because they had so won my heart, that rather than see them upset I would disrupt a family holiday, were responsible for my wife's ultimate realisation of a girlhood dream. Quite sometime after we had been operating the Cattery the whole story came out. When she was a little girl Mimi had been thwarted by grownups who felt that one pet at a time was sufficient. "When I'm all grown up I'll have lots an' lots of cats of my own an' I'll look after other people's cats as well". Well, one little girls dream came true and we would like to share with you the joy and sadness that comes from caring for other people's pets.

2. The Cattery is Born

What I should explain at this point is the fact that we had moved from our original house to a smaller, more modern property just prior to the 'Colditz' incident. The new house was a late 18th Century cottage, the end one of a terrace of three which had in fact all been one property originally, but had been divided between three sisters when they inherited it. There was a large garden to the side and rear of the property and it was in this rear garden that the disused pigeon loft and large greenhouses were to be found.

Our first task was to enclose the rear garden with a dog proof fence to contain our now two Jack Russell terriers - Oonagh and her offspring Mr Woo, son of the original Oscar. Although this is primarily the starting of our Cattery and its visitors, I feel as animal lovers you deserve an explanation as to why a charming, rough haired Jack Russell terrier came by such a name. He is not named after the character in the late George Formby's song, its origin is more complex.

He was, as I said, a charming if somewhat untidy looking rough-coated Jack Russell and the image of his illustrious father. He was, as were his two brothers and two sisters, sent to a new home shortly after weaning. His new owners had a Siamese cat which had been too long the only pet in the household. The newcomer was not welcome and this was made so obvious that the pup was returned to us for his own safety. Rather like the earlier situation with Debbie the inevitable happened, but more quickly, and we acquired another dog. He was incredibly scruffy and despite attempts to give him a suitable name beginning with 'O' as was becoming a tradition he was invariably addressed as 'Scruffy' and this name stuck. The children tended to call him 'Scruffy-wuffy' and this became 'Scruffy-wuffy-woo'. As he matured he became known as 'Mr Woo' although I have to say that until the day he died he was always extremely scruffy.

Back to the main story! The garden was brought into shape and the old kitchen, which was a lean-to affair on the back of the house, demolished, and a large extension containing a mini flat for visiting parents and a new kitchen for us was built.

The salvaged materials from the old kitchen were used to convert the pigeon loft into the garden store eighteen feet by eight feet. The old windows and door were fixed on to the open front and the space in between boarded over with the old roof boards. Even the original nails were used, and in fact to fix the final few boards I was carefully straightening the last few nails and it had become a point of honour not to spend any money on the shed! This was the shed which had the first two cages installed and from which the whole Cattery grew.

There was in fact, as I already indicated, a benevolent conspiracy going on which involved the retired owner of the original cattery and our local Vet. There was a great demand for a good quality cattery in our area and the Vet lost no opportunity in suggesting to Mimi that with her nursing background, her love of animals and her innate common sense she was the ideal person in the ideal place to provide a much needed service to the community. The other co-conspirator, Miss Williams, the retired cattery owner, would ring and say that one of her clients had a particularly sensitive cat and could Mimi possibly help out by taking it in. It soon became obvious that we were to become cattery owners irrespective of whether we wanted to or not!

The old pigeon loft had been part divided internally into three areas and so it was easy to make six spacious cages, each of which looked out on to the garden. We were sure, since the cats that came to us were pets that would appreciate the home environment in preference to a zoo environment, that we should create as much of a 'home' ambience as possible. Our philosophy from the start was that no cat should 'face' another because as territorial animals this could add to the stress of being away from home. All cages should have a view of the garden so that the cats could see movement and bird life and perhaps more importantly, would see us as we worked in the garden. After all if they were pets they would want as much human contact as we could provide.

3. General Behaviour of Cats

We soon learned how diverse is the nature of the cat!

When a cat is left in a cattery it tends to do two things. The first is to make its owner feel as wretched as possible, and the second is to carry out some form of protest to let the cattery owner know who is boss.

One such expert at giving a passable imitation of the Aristos awaiting the Tumbrils was a black cat called - obviously - Lucky. Her owner was a young woman who unfortunately had experienced some bad times with an ill husband, and was now on her own except for Lucky. As a result Lucky was 'spoilt rotten' as they say, nothing was too much trouble for her owner to provide the best most loving home. Lucky by name and Lucky by nature. The owner's mother decided a foreign holiday would be a good boost for the daughter's health and morale, and Lucky would come to us. Mother and daughter both came and we and the Cattery were subjected to a very thorough scrutiny. All was well and Lucky was duly booked to come in the night before departure day. We had quickly learned to tell our customers it is not a good idea to let the cat see you pack, give it breakfast and let it out to have a breath of air! Cats are not silly, they know what a suitcase is for and if they are not allowed to stay in it while it is being packed they soon realise that the holiday plans do not include them. At this point your average feline decides 'Mum' must be taught a short sharp lesson. This is easily achieved by taking off up the nearest tree or failing that getting onto the roof and making oneself comfortable on the ridge tiles.

However, I digress, so to return to Lucky. She duly arrived looking the picture of gloom and when put into the cage in the centrally heated building proceeded to give the aforementioned impersonation of a victim of the terror. Mum was extremely distressed which, of course, was precisely the effect Lucky wanted. I was only too well aware that cats, like children, play the audience for all its worth. Mum calmed down in the house and then I told her to follow my instructions precisely. We made our way silently back to the Cattery, keeping out of Lucky's line of sight. The Cattery was bathed in sunlight and sitting sunning herself in a patch of warmth with a look of absolute bliss was Lucky. Mum was not sure whether to be cross or relieved, but at least she went off in the right frame of mind to enjoy the benefits of her holiday.

Another common form of protest is the boycott technique; this varies from having absolutely nothing to do with us, food or anything, to the more common cold shoulder for the owner but eating a hearty meal when unobserved.

The first time Whiskey came to us was at Easter, which in view of his protest system was perhaps appropriate. All the cats were provided with a fresh cardboard box as a bed unless they brought their own, and into this we usually place some item the owner has brought to give puss a reminder of home. Whiskey came with a large woolly sweater which completely filled the box provided. After the owners had gone we went back with a water bowl and some elevenses and there was no sign of Whiskey. On opening the cage there was still no sign of life, but when we went to move the box to see behind it the weight indicated that someone was indeed in there. For two days we replaced used litter trays and took food dishes in, which were magically emptied when we returned with the next meal. On the third day he arose! Having made his protest, Whiskey now insisted that we make a great fuss and entertain him whenever we went into the building.

There are several variations on the twenty-four or forty-eight hour protest. Sometimes it consists of not emerging from their carrying box, or sometimes the preferred option is to subject us to verbal or physical abuse. This last option is carried to its extreme by one of two beautiful Persian tabbies who have been regular visitors since they were kittens. Bonny is the very model of docility but Bilboe, as I said to his Mum, is "not a happy little Hobbit". He refused to come out of his carrying cage, to change litter trays or clean we in fact had to close him up in his carrying cage. This was done somewhat in the style of a circus lion tamer, the top lid of the cage being shut by prodding it with the locking pole, which was then quickly fitted into place to hold the lid closed. It was still a tricky procedure to put your hand into the pen, because out through the bars of the carrying cage would reach a violently thrashing paw with claws fully extended, all of this being accompanied by the most appalling spitting and swearing from Bilboe.

In all fairness I must say their protests, particularly of the violent kind, were in the minority. Kittens and young cats almost always adapt very easily and quickly to cattery life, after all, when you measure your experiences in months not years then everything that happens to you is new and exciting. The more elderly cats also adapt well, they have seen it all, done it all and one is never surprised by anything. They in fact epitomise the 'laid back dude'.

4. Little Old Ladies

One of the nicest things about running a cattery is that you meet so many charming people of all ages. One tends to get to know the older folks, particularly those who are on their own apart from the cats, perhaps on a more personal basis than those who have families and work colleagues. Like any good business we like to look after our customers and we not only offer a collection and delivery service, we also tend to take cats for their annual 'booster jabs' and other visits to the Vet.

The 'little old ladies' to whom I refer may be either feline or human. I am moving now to some of the sadness we see in our day to day contact with cat folk.

Many elderly ladies have been widowed, and their sole companion is the cat. How often have we heard the phrase "she's all I've got in the world, if anything happens to her I don't know what I'll do." The sense of responsibility when we hear this is tremendous and, of course, the puss in question is often in the 10-20 year age bracket! The other concern so often expressed is for the welfare of the puss if the owner pops off first. There are excellent charities which will help but ideally they should be involved with the owner before their demise.

There are, of course, many 'little old ladies' who are cherished pets and we often are involved with them not only through their lives, but at the end too. I have on occasions taken cats to the Vet to be put to sleep because their lives have become so burdensome, and naturally I have always stayed with the animal, usually holding it in my arms until life is extinct. I have always done this for my own animals as I believe it is important that they are aware of your presence up to the last. Our policy has always been to treat visiting cats as if they were our own. When we return and spend some time with the grieving owner they invariably find it of particular comfort that the animal has been held until the last.

I remember on one occasion I performed this service for one of our long standing customers. I was surprised to realise that the Vet performing the service was quite emotional. He is a very caring man and a cat lover himself but this was obviously different. We had both known the elderly lady owner and the cat for some time and in fact it turned out that 'Fluffy' had been his first patient when he joined the Practice.

This particularly elderly lady owner lived in a house that was built quite literally on rock and had nowhere in her garden to bury her pet. She did not want cremation so we offered to bury her pet. She was most grateful and we chose a spot just below the old stone boundary wall next to a Hazel tree. We carried out the burial and then a little time later the old lady came to tea and we showed her the spot. She was delighted and felt much better about her loss. All this may seem strange to some readers, but I am sure others who have a different view of things will understand. We have since carried out this sad service for several clients over the years.

As you will understand a business such as ours is much more personal than, for instance, a shop where the customers call in off the street and you may or may not see them again. Although we do have a few 'one offs' most clients become regular users often over a period of years. This means that you build up a much more intimate relationship with them than is possible in other businesses. Several clients have, over the years, become firm friends as I will recount later.

The caring aspect of our relationship with clients I have already covered, the extra services we provide, such as collection, delivery and taking animals to the Vet either for treatment or euthanasia. Another aspect is the re-homing of pets when their owners pass away. As you can imagine in a retirement area such as ours many clients are on their own, sometimes with no other relations or with family living quite some distance away. We, therefore, often end up jokingly regarding ourselves as running a Social Services department with a cattery on the side. It is something we are quite happy to do but it does result in us attending an abnormally large number of funerals!

The local Undertaker who we have known for many years is quite used to us appearing at funerals, and usually greets us with "Another client I presume." Often we meet the distant family and are often pleasantly surprised to find they know all about us, and in fact are very pleased to meet us. Sometimes, sadly, we are the only mourners at the service and then we feel particularly pleased to have made the effort to attend.

There are, however, occasions when these particular events can go slightly wrong. I will tell you first of a funeral service that did not go quite according to plan. The client in question had been a long standing user of our services whose cat had died some time previously, and she now needed care at home. We occasionally visited her and one day we received a message from Social Services to say that she had died and that her funeral was on Friday.

We resolved to go as we were fairly certain that she had very few relations, most of whom were themselves elderly. We went to lunch at our regular haunt in a village close to the Crematorium. The Waitress who we knew quite well realised we were not about our normal cattery business because instead of our 'country clothes', we were looking quite respectable. We explained the situation, had lunch and made our way to the funeral service.

When we went in we were rather surprised at the number of mourners because we were under the impression, as I have said that the lady was almost quite alone. We sat unobtrusively at the back and the coffin arrived and the Minister stood and said, "We are gathered here today to remember Mr 'John Doe'." (Obviously I cannot quote the real name). We exchanged horrified glances but sat through the service. We sang the hymns with vigour only to realise that the rest of the mourners were obviously not by any means as familiar as we were with hymns. When the service finished we made our departure as quickly and unobtrusively as possible.

We rang Social Services to find out what had gone wrong and discovered that we were a week early! Naturally we were there the following week, including lunch at our usual place, much to the amusement of our waitress friend. We were glad that we did attend this time as we and her carer were the only mourners.

The other funeral refers to that of a cat and occurred on Easter Monday. As I explained at the beginning of the chapter, we sometimes do the honours for elderly owners. In this case the owner concerned was in fact an elderly neighbour who had been told that her cat, Fred, had been seen lying apparently dead in the garden of a nearby holiday cottage which was closed up for the winter. We went and examined the cat which was very dead. We went to the neighbour who called her relatives to come over. After some discussion, in view of the lack of suitable space we all decided to bury the cat where he fell. I went into the garden of the holiday cottage and dug a grave under the hedge making sure it was good and deep to prevent any risk of foxes getting at the body.

When I returned the family had arrived and were drinking tea and comforting the old lady, when the door slowly opened and in walked Fred. There was a brief moment of shocked silence, and then most appropriately the whole group (strict Baptists all) broke into a rousing chorus of 'Up From the Grave He Arose'. When the rejoicing at the reappearance of Fred calmed down, the question then arose, whose cat had we buried?

There was only one solution, as pet owners ourselves we knew that the true owner would like to know what had happened to their cat. We, therefore, composed a tactfully worded advert to the effect that for information regarding a missing large ginger and white cat please contact the Cattery. This was placed in the window of our local store. In no time at all we had a reply and had to break the sad news to the owners who lived locally.

The wife, understandably, insisted that she wanted to have the body and bury it in her own garden. The problem was she could not be persuaded to wait. It had been raining all day and was beginning to get dark. Her husband and I took ourselves off to disinter the body. However, after twenty-four hours of continuous rain the garden was waterlogged.

Working by torch light we dug out the grave and recovered the body. This simple sentence does not do justice to the Dickensian scene of grave robbers. Imagine if you will a dark, windy night and lashing rain. Two bedraggled, soaking wet figures with wet hair plastered to our heads engaged in the sinister task of disinterring a freshly buried body. The deed was done, and the husband took the body away to try and make it as presentable as possible before taking it home. I was left to fill in the grave and to try and return the hedgerow and adjacent lawn to some semblance of normality. This would have been almost impossible under ideal conditions, I did not have those and in fact despite my best efforts, the garden could well have been used to recreate a trench warfare scene from the 1914-1918 War.

Over the ensuing days I tried to make good the damage with some degree of success, but despite this the relations with the owner were understandably strained. I am happy to say that with time he began to see some humour in the situation.

5. Tale of Blackie

One cat, and owner, I wish to tell you about made the national news in their day. The owner was an elderly lady who had an artificial hip which had a habit of dislocating at the most inopportune moments, and also she had a badly reset wrist fracture. These factors meant that not only did she have great difficulty in moving about, but she also almost always needed emergency hospitalisation each time the hip became dislocated, which invariably occurred at extremely odd hours of the day and night.

She would not leave her flat until 'Blackie' was safe and secure in our Cattery. As a result at any time we could and frequently did receive frantic telephone calls from the ambulance crew asking us to call and collect the cat so that they would take the old lady to hospital. As you might imagine on occasions the very patient and overworked ambulance crew would lose their cool. We always responded as promptly as possible because we were only too well aware of the scene that would greet us. It was like a scene from a Tom and Jerry cartoon film with the old lady giving a very good impersonation of 'Tom', refusing to be put out by being spread eagled with all four feet braced against the door frame. Once Blackie was safely in our care, however, the old lady went like a lamb into the ambulance and off for treatment. This story ends, as I said, with national news coverage as I will now relate.

One Sunday morning just before lunch we received a telephone call from the local newspaper and the reporter asked about a legacy we had been left. We knew nothing of this, but as Wills are public documents newspapers apparently routinely receive information of any substantial or unusual bequests. The bequest in question was both substantial and unusual. We had been left the cat 'Blackie' who was to live in the Cattery for the rest of her life and she, 'Blackie' had been left the sum of £50,000 to pay boarding and vet's fees.

I jokingly said to a friend who was having lunch with us that we would surely be on the front page of the Western Morning News on Monday and thought no more about it as I opened the wine to have with our lunch. We had in fact only just finished our lunch when a second telephone call from the paper asked for us to receive a photographer and reporter within the hour. They arrived and after chatting for a while we were photographed, along with Blackie who we had brought into the house. We were quite prepared to accept the fees for her keep, but had decided it would be kinder to bring her into the household and introduce her to our current dog and three cats.

My joking remark to our friend proved to be most prophetic and in fact a quarter-page picture and report did appear on the front page of the paper. This was at the time of the first Gulf War and inside the paper was a single column with a picture of Saddam Hussein. Who says the Western Morning News hasn't got its priorities right?

We had no sooner got over the shock of the newspaper report when the telephone started to ring. Appointments were made for the BBC, ITV, and BBC Radio Devon to come later that day.

The first TV team duly arrived, they shot some footage of the entrance to the Cottage, taking in the various stone cats which adorn the entrance. We were then filmed going about the normal business of the Cattery which was followed by an interview with Mimi. This took place in the conservatory which we use as a reception area for clients. Mimi was on the settee, the reporter stood to one side, and the camera man crouched in the opposite corner. The interview went very well with Blackie on Mimi's knee. To give dramatic effect to Blackie's newfound wealth we had, at the request of the interviewer, put a silver bracelet on her as a collar. The first part involved taking some shots of Mimi nodding and smiling, this was to be spliced in when the reporter was speaking. Then the interview began, and soon the inevitable question arose, "How do the animals get on with the new arrival?" Mimi had just said that they were all settling in well together when something upset the apple cart as it were. A tremendous scrap broke out; the camera man stepped back and tripped. He ended up amongst the various plants in the corner, the interviewer collapsed into uncontrollable laughter and if chaos did not reign it certainly had a working majority. In the fullness of time order was restored and the interview proceeded. It was rounded off with a shot of Blackie in her silver collar tasting smoked salmon! When it was shown on TV the whole interview as always looked smooth, well conducted and polished. If only the viewers knew the truth!

The first TV crew had not been gone long when a team from the other channel arrived. The interview was along the same lines but they obviously felt that they needed an alternative 'angle' to their rivals. After similar questions they ended the interview showing our other cats, two Birmans and finally the big ginger 'Mr Rupert'. He was shown studying a bank savings book and the final question was, "Are the boys interested in Blackie or her bank account?" Immediately the following day our bank manager telephoned to thank us for the free publicity for his bank. Sadly he did not reduce our overdraft.

In the evening, both TV channels and BBC Radio Devon carried the story. We were, of course, quite exhausted and had no food in the house we, therefore, went to our usual pub for a meal. The landlord who we had known for many years made a great show of our arrival, and we suffered quite a ribbing from him and all the regulars who wanted autographs etc from the latest TV celebrities. We were very surprised at the response from the media but they explained that there was so much bad news about that contrary to popular belief, they were delighted to report on a story with a happy ending.

The story in fact went world-wide and some of our clients on holiday in the Canary Islands saw our picture in full colour on the front of a German magazine, and were able to bask in the reflected glory of knowing us and Blackie.

Blackie lived with us for many years and became a fully integrated member of the household so she was able to live out her life in comfort and ease.

6. Collection and Delivery

As I mentioned earlier, we offer to our clients a collection and delivery service. Most people like to bring their pets, to see them settled and to discuss with us their likes and dislikes and their odd habits. I shall tell of likes, dislikes and odd habits later, but for the moment tell of two of the most unusual incidents of collection.

Most collections go fairly smoothly, there may be some chasing around to catch the cat but usually this is considered part of the job. On one occasion I feel we had to go beyond the normal bounds of duty. It had been a particularly trying and arduous day involving the collection or return of several cats over a fairly large area of the county. We were both tired and hungry and hoped to snatch a meal before the final arrival planned for later that evening.

This was not to be, we arrived home to find an answer phone message from a new client asking if we could come and collect her cat immediately, as her car had broken down. We took time for a quick cup of tea then made our way out into the winter night to find the house of the new owner. Unfortunately, it turned out to be a rather obscure part of town with which we were not familiar and on a dark, wet evening it took some finding.

We eventually arrived, to be greeted by a less than friendly owner who asked us to hurry as they were waiting to have their evening meal. Biting back uncharitable thoughts we followed her into the house, only to be told that the cat had disappeared behind the kitchen units! The owner was unable to coax her pet out and this meant that there were only two alternatives, we either left the cat where it was or dismantle enough of the kitchen to get at it. As is usual on these occasions the owner had left collection until the last moment and had very little time left to get to the airport.

You have guessed it! Out to the car for my tools I went, and started to take the kitchen apart. At least we were able to persuade the owner that it was a job best left to us, experience has shown that hysterical anxious owners create hysterical anxious cats, and that was the last thing we wanted. After summing up the situation we closed off all possible re-entry points to the spaces behind the units and did some quick dismantling work. Within twenty minutes we had the cat secure in our own carrying box and the kitchen returned to normal. It was only then we allowed the owner back. Needless to say we did not open the box to allow the owner one last goodbye cuddle!

We have always prided ourselves with giving owners the best possible service, and my wife runs the whole operation as efficiently as a hospital Matron, except on one occasion - not bad for over thirty years in business. The 'occasion' needs recording not just for its rarity value but because it also illustrates the slightly bizarre world in which we animal lovers exist.

We had invited to dinner the Chemistry Master from our son's old prep school. We had not seen him for many years but had recently met him and heard he had just married. He was anxious to know how Tim, our son, was getting on and we thought it would be a nice gesture to invite him and his new wife to dinner and reminisce with him.

They duly arrived and all was going along quite well when the telephone rang. This was not uncommon, and as my wife was in the process of fetching dessert from the kitchen she took the call in there. She eventually came in looking a little flustered and upset to tell us it was an elderly lady who was getting quite concerned as to what time we were going for her cat. For the first time in twenty-odd years we had forgotten about a collection! As the client was an elderly lady and it was late at night, my wife said she would quickly nip out and make the collection, which was from a house no more than a quarter of a mile away. As none of the puddings on offer were hot, we who were remaining there said we would happily await her return.

After some twenty minutes had elapsed, and conversation was faltering because we were all beginning to become a little anxious, in came a very disheveled Mimi. She had left the house looking more elegant than lady cattery owners normally do, dressed in long skirt and white blouse. She returned, minus the cat, hair awry and her blouse covered with so much blood she looked like a victim of the Texas chainsaw massacre!

The cat was a large powerful British Rex who had made it very plain it did not want to go into a carrying box nor into a cattery. There seemed no alternative but for us both having to go to collect this particular cat. With a cheerful, "talk amongst yourselves" to our dinner guests we set off. Fortunately with two of us, the cat was quickly brought under control and safely boxed up. We took him back, installed him safely in a cage and returned to continue our meal, but not before Mimi had carried out some instant repairs to her appearance and changed into non-blood stained garments.

Strangely, for some reason, the dinner party did not really recover and our guests beat a fairly hasty retreat. We do hope all is well with them as we have not seen them since!

7. Cats and Their Strange Ways

As I have mentioned earlier, cats have ways of protesting and making their owner feel particularly bad about leaving them. I have already said about cats hiding, they will also refuse food for a time. This in itself is not a worry so long as it is a twenty-four or forty-eight hour protest, but if it becomes more prolonged it can be a concern because cats can deteriorate quite rapidly if left alone under these circumstances.

Obviously the first thing to do is to try and tempt them with a favourite food or even some new taste. Sometimes smearing a small amount of Marmite on their noses will start them off, once they lick some of the vitamin B12 in the Marmite this will be sufficient to give them an appetite. If these various methods do not work then our usual policy is to take them to our Vet who gives them a B12 injection. This usually sets them on the way and then there are no further problems, although occasionally we have had a cat which only manages a sustenance diet. This is the one source of protest which always does concern us when carried to excess.

We did have one cat which stayed with us which carried the 'food fad' to extremes. It was a very well bred cat with an impeccable pedigree. In fact it was so well bred that if it could talk it would not speak to the likes of us! It belonged to some good friends of ours and we were all most concerned about its voluntary starvation. We tried all the normal methods to get it to eat but to no avail. It had only been staying for long weekends so we had not felt it necessary to resort to the B12 injections from the Vet. Eventually it was due in for a longer stay and we had all agreed that if we had no result after four days we would have to use the Vet.

When the cat arrived we were all quite anxious to avoid a trip to the Vet's. Mike, the owner, joked that if all else failed Max, the cat, would always eat smoked salmon. It so happened that a friend from Ireland had brought some, so we tried this on day two for breakfast. Max wolfed it down! He then tackled a plate of normal cat food. The next day we fed him his normal diet and he ate this with enthusiasm. We always have, when possible, a means of contacting the owners and in this case we did. We rang them and told them the tale of Max's eating habits. They were, of course, delighted and as a result were able to enjoy the rest of their holiday safe in the knowledge that Max was eating well and was quite content on his 'hols'.

Another form of protest which we have observed is a reluctance to leave their carrying boxes. It has always been our policy to place the carrying box in the cage and let the cat emerge in its own time. On one occasion a cat had come out to explore, but before I could remove the box I was called away to the telephone. On my return the cat had gone back into its carrying box. I left it and went on with other jobs, coming back at intervals intending to remove the box. The cat remained in the box and even slept there. It had in fact been inclined to scratch when the cage was cleaned, but now was completely docile. We had also noticed that although the cats did not always like to be boxed up at home, they were invariably very happy to go into the carrying boxes to go home. We began to suspect that when they saw the box at home they associated it with either a visit to the vet or to the cattery, neither of which they particularly liked. However, when they were at the cattery then it meant they were going home. We then found that about 40% of them preferred the box left in their cages, some would use it day and night to rest or sleep in and some would rest in a conventional bed during the day and retire at night to the box. We now leave the box in the cage unless the cat makes it quite obvious, which they do, that it prefers a normal bed only in the cage.

We provide suitable beds for all our visitors if they want them. Originally we gave them each a new cardboard box, but as numbers grew we found it better to use easily sterilised plastic beds. We provide several thicknesses of newspaper as insulation and encourage the owner to bring their own blankets or perhaps a sweater from home as the familiar smell is of comfort to the cat. Sometimes this desire to remind their pets of home can be carried to extremes. We had one owner who always brought with them a potted palm and a piece of carpet similar to that in their living room. Apparently the cat spends its time sitting in the window under the palm looking at the wildlife in the garden. Personally I think cats are quite bright, and can imagine the cat thinking to itself, *Who do they think they are fooling? Don't they realise I can recognise my own garden?* Although I am inclined to feel the cat was not fooled, like it, I was prepared to humour the owner!

8. Other Cat Habits

As I have said, most cats settle in quite quickly and prove no problem at all. Many who are regular visitors do seem to enjoy their 'holiday', particularly if there are young children in the household. I think they enjoy a bit of peace and quiet!

One interesting thing we have found with a few cats is that when we are in the garden and they are watching, they really do respond to a smile and a wave. This is normally in the form of a shake of the head or a meow of some sort. We have, however, had two cats which have responded in a very positive way. They wave! Not as an adult would but if you will think about a small baby, when asked to wave they often raise a hand and then open and close it. Both the cats to which I refer did just that. They would raise a paw to head height and then open and close it.

On the first occasion I saw this I assumed it was a coincidence, but when I repeated the exercise and received a 'wave' in reply I rushed in to Mimi and told her. I was somewhat deflated when she casually said, "Oh yes, Maisie always does that when you wave at her". The owner was particularly pleased when we confirmed this happening because she was then able to convince her somewhat cynical husband that she was not going barmy.

There are many other little idiosyncrasies that cats have and I will tell you of a few more, some nice, some not so nice. I have already mentioned hiding and beds and this is fairly normal but can sometimes be carried to extreme lengths. We have several cats who have 'igloo' type beds which not only provide warmth and shelter, but also a degree of a challenge. An easy trick for a beginner is to jump up and down on the igloo and create a 'normal' shaped bed instead. The next variation is to remove the interior cushion, create a normal bed and then place the cushion in this. The real expert, however, can turn the bed completely inside out and then reinstall the cushion.

One less sanitary aspect to the above tricks is, of course, to use the cushion for an entirely different purpose. It will make an excellent cover for a litter tray. If you are a tidy minded cat, when you have used your tray you cover it with the cushion from your bed. This is not too bad, but if your tidiness is combined with a degree of absent mindedness you may decide to sleep on your cushion. The effect I will not describe in detail, cat owners amongst you will know and understand. Non-cat owners do not need to have their sensibilities upset by details!

Another aspect of cats is that whilst they are invariably elegant and exhibit considerable grace of movement they can be incredibly clumsy. This clumsiness does not manifest itself often. Normally it occurs on two main occasions, the first and most amusing is when a young cat has started learning to hunt. It will be bold and unafraid; it will probably be prepared to attack a full grown butterfly or even a dragonfly. It is the latter which is usually its downfall.

Dragonflies, as you well know, tend to be around ponds. Rest assured that your young cat will demonstrate its complete fearlessness by taking a giant leap at its prey. Unfortunately it is unlikely to have thought the whole exercise through. You have guessed it! The landing, usually without the dragonfly, will be in the deepest part of the pond. A variation on this is walking onto a lily pad in pursuit of a stranded tadpole. Unless this happens to be one of those giant leaves at Kew Gardens the result is somewhat similar to the dragonfly incident.

The second occasion when cats demonstrate their clumsiness is best dealt with quickly! It is when they decide to walk along a display shelf full of precious ornaments. At least two will crash to the ground, and they will be the most cherished.

I personally had an example of this one night. I was sleeping in the living room and our new kitten was also there. In the early hours of the morning she suddenly decided that she could leap from the bed settee onto the mantle shelf. She could, unfortunately she grabbed a brass candle stick on landing. This toppled off the shelf, bounced off my head and landed in the hearth with an almighty clatter. I woke, somewhat confused, only to be confronted by a three month old Birman kitten. Her view was "Hurrah, Dad is awake we can have a game." As you have probably gathered by now I am a patient (beaten?) man, so a game we had.

We have also noticed that some cats have a sense of humour. Some have a remarkable sense of what is expected of them. The first situation is best illustrated by describing the sort of antics which can occur. This, which in fact is more play than sense of humour, is the type of cat, and there are many, who will sit patiently in its bed whilst you talk to it as you clean its cage. It is usually only the youngsters who like to go out into the 'playground' while you clean their cages, most others prefer a chat while you work. When you have got all the litter which invariably finds it way on to the cage floor in a nice neat pile ready to be swept into the dust pan, then the previously indolent cat suddenly comes to life.

A series of swift somersaults through the pile will scatter it all over the cage again. If they are really skilled operators they can also considerably invert the water bowl into the mess. This means that now a second cleaning operation is necessary involving cloths, tissues and such like to gather up the resultant 'gunge'. Believe me, if you are a cat this is much more entertaining than hunting spiders in the ivy clad sides of the play area.

A real sense of humour is shown by some cats when you walk by their cage. Just as you have passed they will flick water from their drinking bowls on to the back of your neck. This is definitely a deliberate act and is done by a small but significant number of our guests.

I think one small interesting point to mention here, which tends to support my feeling that some cats at least show a remarkable ability to relate to humans, is the tale of Rupert.

9. The Tale of Rupert and Perkins

Rupert was a classic example of the "Ginger Tom from next door" as a famous comedian used to say. He came to us originally as a guest named 'Binky'. He was owned by two Dutch gentlemen who had a residence in the town. One or other of them was almost always here but if they both needed to be away at the same time then 'Binky', who was much loved by both his owners, came to us.

As time went on the older of the owners succumbed to alcoholism and became more and more of a hazard to 'Binky'. Sometimes 'Binky' would be left out and forgotten when his owner went off for a few days. This was not satisfactory, of course, but at least he was able to shelter in the garden shed or greenhouse. A much worse situation was if he was locked in the house the whole time the owner was away. The younger partner, because of the older man's problems, was forced to spend more and more time in Holland looking after their business interests. Eventually it became obvious that the situation could not continue and they asked us to take 'Binky' into our family.

This we did but it did present some problems. 'Binky' had become very wary of people and needed reassurance. He integrated well with our three other cats, the two Birmans I have already mentioned, and also Perkins who had belonged to my wife's mother, who had recently died. We also had a Lakeland-Patterdale terrier cross named Mr Oliver. The first meeting of 'Binky' and Mr Oliver was quite humorous to see. Oliver was quite used to cats as you can imagine, so in his usual amiable way he strolled over to say "hello". He was met with a powerful left hook from 'Binky'. Being a perfect gentleman he merely took it literally on the chin, shrugged and wandered off looking slightly confused. 'Binky', having made his point, got along perfectly well with them all. I should explain perhaps that this tale is about how adaptable cats are and that 'Binky' was in fact renamed soon after his permanent installation into our household as 'Rupert the Red'.

One other problem which must have occurred during the latter stages of his stay with the original owners, which probably precipitated his arrival with us, was that he must have been kicked and trodden on when the owner was very drunk. Rupert was very sensitive about being touched or lifted and he would react quite violently. We spent much time with him reassuring him that we would not hurt him in any way. This was eventually so successful that not only could you pet him, but also pick him up and even nurse him in your arms like a baby. This shows how cats can adapt to the right situation and have a very happy life which Rupert did for many years.

Perkins, who I mentioned earlier, had another way of coping with the sudden change in her circumstances when my wife's mother died. We brought Perkins home and she was quite overwhelmed by the presence of two playful Birman cats and a very boisterous terrier. She found the cats' approach too much for an elderly lady cat who had led a quiet life. As for Mr Oliver, she had never met such a thing before and was very frightened, because she did not know he was in fact a most gentle dog who loved cats having been brought up with the Birmans. They loved him, but used to take advantage of his gentle nature and take some dreadful liberties with him. Their favourite game was to get him to chase them up and down the stairs, then Bunty, the smaller one would drop down onto a stair and as Mr O charged down she would catch his front paw. This would result in an undignified tumble down the remaining stairs for him. He was a very bright dog and I am convinced he knew it was coming but humoured these two girls by 'taking a dive' as they expected.

As a result of all this mayhem, poor Perkins retired

to the bathroom and lived there for several weeks with her food being taken up to her. After some four or five weeks she appeared one morning in the kitchen. She strolled in, settled down on a convenient chair and when Mr O, who was always a late riser, came in they both behaved as if she had always lived here and calm was restored. I hope these two tales illustrate that with patience and time cats can adapt and become happy members of a peaceful loving home.

10. Survivors

After telling you how well cats can adapt to a new home and owners, I feel two stories of how cats can survive traumatising injuries and still become loving and trusting pets are worth repeating.

The first instance involves an accident. It happened at the Britannia Royal Naval College where a stray cat had found what she thought was a good, safe place to have her kittens.

She crept into a warm, dark part of the building and unbeknown to her she then chose a boiler firebox to give birth. She duly did so and started to rear her kittens.

The weather became colder, and it became necessary to fire up additional boilers to augment the heating system. As the boiler was fired up a terrified cat burst from the fire door. It was terribly burned and sadly the kittens were lost. The staff managed to catch the cat and smother the flames. They then rushed her to the local vet whose first instinct was to put her down and end her misery. The Naval College staff asked him if possible to sedate her and then help them to restore her to health. The Officers and men of the college covered all the costs and with patience and care she was restored to full health, although she was an odd looking creature since both ears had been reduced to stumps, and her new fur was fairly short and curly.

She repaid their care by becoming a most loving pet, and to prevent any further harm coming to her she was adopted by one of the staff who was able to provide her with a caring home. She stayed with us when the family holidayed, and she was a lovely character who did not appear to suffer any long term problems from her ordeal.

That was the story of a cat which survived a terrible accident and through care and affection recovered well.

The next story is in some ways worse, as it shows the mindless violence which is sometimes handed out to animals - and sadly to people as well.

A lovely little Tortoiseshell cat was taken from a rescue centre into the home of a very caring couple who were giving it a good life. One day they returned home to find that thieves had broken in. They had ransacked the house but much worse had attacked the cat so viciously that it was so severely injured that once again, the Vet was inclined to put her down.

The couple concerned were not willing to do this without giving their beloved pet a chance. The first thing was to attempt to deal with her injuries and this involved amputation of a front leg. The cat was then treated with medication and much care by the owners. With time, it made a good recovery and is now one of the most popular visitors to the Cattery. The amazing thing to us is that despite the terrible trauma from this attack it is such a gentle, loving and trusting little cat who wins the hearts of all who meet her.

It is so amazing that these animals recover not only physically but mentally from these terrible experiences and go on to lead happy and contented lives.

You see, what could have been a depressing chapter shows that the vast majority of people are good and kindly souls, and our pets recognise this and respond to it.

11. Favourites (Or What You Shouldn't Have)

Cats, like people, are all different. This means that although they are all treated with the same care and kindness, some will respond more positively than others. There, that's my excuse for having favourites.

First to generalise, there are two groups which provide the most favourites: the young and the very old. In the case of the former everything is new and exciting, they are playful and inquisitive. The latter have seen it all, done it all and - as the saying goes - got the tee shirt!

All kittens are fun but those which have been well handled from birth can be particularly attractive and usually grow into very affectionate cats. The trick, not just with cats, but in fact with all pets is to release them the moment they want to go. Never insist on cuddling a struggling animal, give it its freedom. Eventually it will come to you for cuddles because it enjoys it but knows it will not be restricted. As I mentioned earlier when telling you about Rupert, it can take time and patience but you will be well rewarded eventually.

We have one young cat which comes to us that has a particularly lovely nature and lives in an ideal home for pets. He nearly was not so fortunate, one of the children developed a rash and the family GP said "get rid of the cat". The owner was very distressed, as was the child. I enquired if any tests had been done as to why the child should suddenly develop the rash when the cat had been with them for some considerable time. The owner said there was no discussion or anything other than what can only be described as a 'knee jerk' reaction by the GP. My advice was to wait and see. The rash cleared of its own accord, the child and the cat continued to be healthy and happy. This has now grown into a beautiful natured cat which not only us but also visiting clients find so friendly.

The adult cats we tend to favour as a generality are ginger. I do not know why but they almost always are large, laid back characters. Dare I say it may be because they are male! We did have one exception, a big ginger ex-farm cat who had had a most dreadful time. He is one of the three cats who have managed to inflict serious damage on me in over thirty years of animal care. Sadly he died not long after he was rescued but he was already making progress, and had learned to trust his owners.

We had another ginger who was in one of the small group of cats which are almost clowns in their behaviour. They literally throw themselves on their backs and kick their legs in the air whenever they see you. They lie in their beds with a paw dropped elegantly over side and so obviously pose that it is hard not to be captivated by them.

12. The Other Side of the Coin

I may, during the writing of this book, have gone on about what we do for cats or their owners. I feel it is very important to acknowledge all that owners do for us.

As I have said before, this business is a long term relationship with clients, many of whom have become friends. Quite often they will bring small 'thank you' gifts, but the most humbling and rewarding came when I was suddenly struck down with a debilitating illness. One day I was a very fit man, the next I was unable to climb stairs or do much else.

Within days we were inundated with offers of practical help of all kinds:

"I'll help in the cattery,"

"I'll take Don to the hospital,"

"Do you need any shopping?"

These offers were not made lightly but with a genuine desire to help, as was proven during the following months. As a result some very firm friendships were forged during what was for my wife a very trying and frightening time. I am not naming names, not only because these folk would be embarrassed, but also in case I miss any out. (They would not accept my brain surgery as an excuse for forgetting!) Apart from all this there was also spiritual support - many folks of all religious persuasions prayed for us. This meant a great deal to us as people of faith ourselves.

We had so many cards wishing us well that, as they say, 'we could have papered a room'. The conservatory resembled a florist's shop. The situation eventually resolved itself, and thanks to a brilliant brain surgeon and all the support, I am finally back to normal.

There was one incident which occurred during my recovery period which I must tell you about. We have always been a happy and cheerful family, and our friends share a similar sense of the ridiculous. I was learning to balance again and to walk without the aid of sticks. I wanted to try and 'do my bit' in the Cattery. On this occasion I had made the mid-morning drinks for Mimi and two of her friends. The three of them are all fairly small ladies and were all scrubbing out empty cages. This involved them crawling partly into them, I came into the building to tell them of my achievement and was confronted with three rather shapely female posteriors all moving in a somewhat disturbing way. When I pointed out that this was nearly too much for a chap in my delicate condition they all burst into delighted laughter. This I feel explains to some extent why we enjoy what we do so much – it's fun!

That, however, is not the end of the story. Some time later when I was well on the road to recovery, Mimi was diagnosed with breast cancer. Our world rocked on its axis again. No sooner did they hear then all our friends old and new rallied round again.

Whilst Mimi was in hospital we worked out amongst us a new routine. I would feed the cats, take Mr Darcy (our current dog) for a good run, then return to clean out the cages with the assistance from one of our friends.

I would then go to the hospital, taking Mr Darcy, where he would wait in the car while I had lunch with Mimi. I would then take Mr D for walk, he would return to the car and await one of his two chauffeurs. They would arrive at around 4 p.m. and he would have his harness fitted, and would then be installed in the back seat. He was quite amusing to see, as he would sit up fully alert and one almost expected him to say "carry on driver!" In fact one friend said she was quite surprised that he did not do the 'royal wave'.

So once again, thanks to all our friends we got through another of life's little trials. I hope you have managed to wade through this final chapter, because to us it indicates the huge pleasure to be had from this kind of business if you are of the right temperament. You won't make much money perhaps, but you will have a full and a fun life.